All About
Hamsters

Rachel McKay

Let's learn about hamsters!

What Are Hamsters?	1
What Do Hamsters Eat?	3
Hamsters in the Wild	7
Hamster Cages	9
When do Hamsters Sleep?	13
Hamsters Having Fun	15
Do Hamsters Hibernate?	19
1 Hamster or 2 ?	21
Baby Hamsters	23

What are Hamsters?

Hamsters belong to a class of mammals known as **Rodents**

1

The most common types of pet hamsters are:

Syrian Hamsters

Roborovski Hamsters

Russian Dwarf Hamsters

Did you know? There are **24** different species of hamsters!

Different species of hamsters...

→ have different types of fur

→ behave differently

→ can be different size

Pet hamsters and wild hamsters have some of the same instincts, and behaviours, but they live very different lives!

What Do Hamsters Eat?

For your hamster to be healthy, it's super important that they have the right diet!

Muesli

Some pet hamsters get most of the energy they need from their muesli mix.

But muesli isn't as healthy for hamsters as pellets are.

This is because they might only eat the bits they like, and not get the range of nutrients they need.

Pellets

Pellets are the healthiest way for pet hamsters to get the energy and nutrients they need.

The only problems is- some hamsters don't like them!

Healthy Treats For Hamsters

As well as their pellets or muesli, hamsters always like some healthy treats!

Healthy treats for hamsters include:

small pieces of carrot

a few peas

a couple of pumpkin seeds

Giving your hamster a treat that isn't good for them could make them very ill, so before you give them anything, make sure that it's safe.

Cheek Pouches

Hamsters love to collect and store food!

They carry their food around in large pouches inside their cheeks

They also carry bedding

These cheek pouches can stretch out to the sides, and back to a hamsters shoulders.

Hamsters can store up to **half of their own weight** in food in their cheek pouches.

Hamsters in the Wild

Wild hamsters look different from pet hamsters because they have to be more camouflaged.

Wild Hamsters

- have to search for all of their own food

- have to rely on their instincts to survive

- live in warm, dry areas

Instinct?

Something that an animal just knows to do, without having to learn, or think about it first.

Wild syrian hamsters live completely alone and hardly ever see another hamster.

Some species (like russian dwarf hamsters), live in groups. They do this so that they can help each other find food and warn each other of any danger.

Hamster Cages

One of the most important things you can do for your pet hamster is to give them the right size of cage!

Hamster Cages

Hamsters need to have lots and lots of space to scurry around and play!

80cm

50 cm

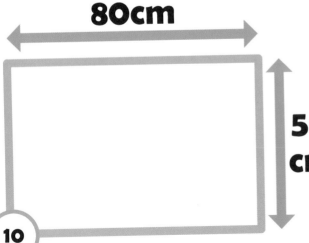

10

Hamsters need a space of at least 80cm x 50cm so they can be healthy.

Small Cages

If a hamster's cage is too small they won't get enough exercise. This means that are more likely to get unwell.

This also means that they'll get bored because they don't have enough space to explore.

If your hamster lives in a small cage, they need a bigger one as soon as possible!

The Perfect Cage

A big floor space → **So they have plenty of space to run around in, and to make space for lots of toys!**

So they can have lots of bedding to dig around in ← **A tall base**

A small space between the bars  → **So they can't squeeze out and get themselves hurt**

When Do Hamsters Sleep?

If you have a pet hamster, you've probably noticed that you hardly ever see them. This is because they sleep during the day.

Nocturnal Creatures

Nocturnal?

Nocturnal animals stay awake at night and sleep during the day.

Hamsters can see a lot better during the night, than they can during the day.

Hamsters like to curl up under lots of bedding to go to sleep.

When a hamster is sleeping, they don't like to be disturbed, so try to leave your hamster alone until they wake up themselves.

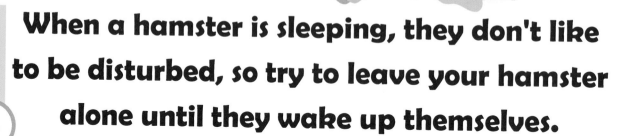

Hamsters

Having

Fun!

Hamsters love to have fun!

Hamsters are very intelligent animals and they need to keep very busy so they don't get bored.

Hamsters don't play together so they do other things to have fun!

Did you know?
Without enough things to do hamsters can get very, very stressed!

To have fun, hamsters love to...

climb run dig gnaw

Hamster Wheels

Hamsters love to run and run and run on their wheel!

Younger hamsters can run for longer than older ones

?

Did you know?

Hamsters can run several miles a night on their wheel.

!

If a hamster's wheel is too small, they have to bend their back to run. This can give them a very sore back.

Hamster Toys

Giving hamsters lots
of different toys to play
with will help to them keep
happy and healthy!

Hamsters
like shelters
and tunnels to
crawl under
and through.

They like ramps
and bridges to run along.

Hamsters like to have
ladders and steps to
climb up and down.

Do Hamsters Hibernate?

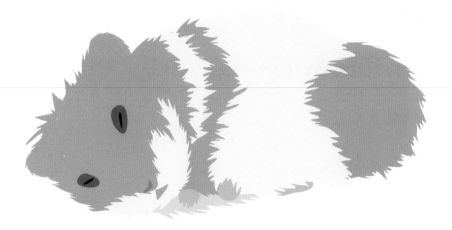

Some animals hibernate to help them survive during the winter. Some wild hamsters hibernate, but pet hamsters don't!

Hibernate?

An animal's heart rate slows down and their temperature drops. This happens when they get too cold or there's not enough food.

Pet hamsters aren't meant to hibernate, so when it looks like they're hibernating they're in 'torpor'.

 Torpor

- Their heart rate and breathing slows down.
- Their temperature drops.
- They need to be gently warmed up

Torpor is dangerous for hamsters.

1 Hamster or 2?

Most hamsters live alone, but some people let their hamsters live together. So, should hamsters live together, or not?

Should hamsters live together?

Syrian hamsters have to live alone, or they will fight and seriously hurt each other.

It's usually best for hamsters to live on their own.

Some dwarf hamsters can live together, but they're still likely to fight. It's better to keep them them apart just in case.

If hamsters start fighting they need to be separated immediately!

Baby Hamsters

Baby hamsters are born without fur, and they can't hear or see. So how do they get from being like this, to being a full grown adult hamster?

Female hamsters can have litters of anywhere from **1-20** babies at a time.

By 7 days old, they can start to move around

By 2 weeks old they can open their eyes

By 3 -4 weeks old they don't need their mother's milk anymore, and they can eat their own food.

They then feed these babies until they are **3-4 weeks old**

After this they need to be separated from their babies or they wil fight with them.

Hamster babies are also called pups.

Looking for more books like this one? Visit

www.allabouthamsters.co.uk

Printed in Great Britain
by Amazon

27401208R00016